THE SHADOW OF THE WHITE CAP

TRUE STORY OF ABDUCTION AND KILLING OF YOUNG JURNALIST

JALIYA RATHNAYAKE

To the courageous parents who refused to be silenced,
To the mothers and fathers who carried the unbearable
weight of loss,
To those who searched endlessly for answers in the face
of fear,
And to the voices that rose above the darkness,
demanding justice for the
disappeared youth of Sri Lanka during the 1987/91
insurrection—

This book is for you.

Your resilience, love, and unyielding pursuit of truth
inspire us all. May your stories remind the world that
even in the face of unimaginable pain, the fight for
justice and dignity endures.

Contents

Preface

This is a story born out of grief, courage, and an unrelenting pursuit of justice. It is a story of a mother's love for her son, a love so fierce that it defied the oppressive forces of a system designed to silence her. It is also a story of a nation in turmoil, where the lines between justice and power blur, and where the truth is often buried beneath layers of fear and complicity.

Set against the backdrop of Sri Lanka in the late 1980s and early 1990s, a time marked by civil unrest, political violence, and state-sponsored terror, this novel is inspired by the real-life tragedy of Richard de Zoysa, a journalist, poet, and activist whose life was brutally cut short. His abduction and murder sent shockwaves through the country, exposing the dark underbelly of a regime that sought to crush dissent at any cost. But this is not just Richard's story—it is the story of his mother, Dr. Manorani Saravanamuttu, who refused to let his death be forgotten.

Through her unwavering determination, Dr. Saravanamuttu became a symbol of resistance, a voice for the voiceless in a time when silence was the safest option. Her fight for justice was not just for her son but for the countless others who had disappeared, their fates unknown, their families left to mourn in silence. Her journey is one of heartbreak and resilience, of despair and hope, of a mother's refusal to let the truth be buried.

This novel is a work of fiction, but it is deeply rooted in the realities of Sri Lanka's history. The characters, events, and settings are inspired by true stories, though they have been fictionalized to explore the emotional and psychological depths of those who lived through these times. It is not just a recounting of events but an attempt to capture the human cost of political violence and the enduring strength of those who fight for justice.

As you read this story, you will walk alongside Dr. Saravanamuttu as she faces unimaginable loss, relentless threats, and a system designed to protect the powerful. You will witness her moments of despair and her flashes of hope, her quiet strength and her fiery resolve. And through her journey, you will see the power of love and truth in the face of oppression.

This novel is dedicated to all those who have fought for justice in the face of insurmountable odds, to the families of the disappeared, and to the memory of Richard de Zoysa, whose voice was silenced but whose legacy endures. May this story serve as a reminder that even in the darkest of times, there are those who refuse to give up, who refuse to be silenced, and who continue to fight for a better world.

CHAPTER ONE

THE ABDUCTION

The city of Colombo, once a bustling hub of trade and culture, had become a shadow of its former self. The streets were eerily quiet after dark, the usual hum of life replaced by the distant rumble of military vehicles and the occasional crack of gunfire. Checkpoints dotted the roads, manned by soldiers with weary eyes and fingers that lingered too long on the triggers of their rifles. The people moved quickly, heads down, avoiding eye contact, as if fear itself had become a contagion.

It was February 18, 1990, and the air was heavy with the kind of silence that only comes before something terrible. In a modest but well-kept home on the outskirts of the city, Dr. Manorani Saravanamuttu sat in her study, the soft glow of a desk lamp illuminating the pages of a medical journal. She had always been a woman of quiet strength, her life dedicated to healing others, but tonight her mind was elsewhere.

Her son, Richard de Zoysa, had gone to bed early. He was leaving for Portugal in a few days, a fresh start that she had encouraged but secretly dreaded. Richard was no ordinary young man. At thirty-one, he had already made a name for himself as a journalist, poet, and actor. His words carried weight, and his voice had become a beacon for those who had none. But in a country where speaking the truth was a dangerous act, his courage had made him a target.

The clock on the wall ticked past three in the morning. Dr. Saravanamuttu rubbed her eyes and closed the journal, deciding it was time to get some rest. She had just stood up when the sound of heavy boots on the gravel driveway froze her in place.

She listened, her heart pounding. The sound grew louder, closer, until it was right outside the front door. A sharp knock echoed through the house, followed by a voice.

"Police! Open the door!"

She hesitated, her mind racing. Why would the police come at this hour? And why did their voices sound so cold, so devoid of humanity?

Before she could move, the door burst open, the lock splintering under the force of a boot. A group of men stormed in, their faces shadowed but their intent unmistakable. One of them, dressed in a white T-shirt, white shorts, and a white cap, stepped forward. His face was pockmarked, his eyes hard and unyielding.

"Where is your son?" he demanded, his voice sharp and commanding.

Dr. Saravanamuttu's breath caught in her throat. "What do you want with him?" she asked, her voice trembling but resolute.

"We need to speak to him," the man said curtly. "Where is he?"

She stepped in front of him, her small frame dwarfed by his imposing presence. "There's no need to take him downstairs," she said, her voice firm despite the fear that gripped her.

The man in the white cap ignored her. He pushed past her, his boots thudding against the wooden floor as he made his way to Richard's room.

"Amma?" Richard's voice called out, groggy and confused. He appeared in the doorway, his hair disheveled, his eyes widening as he took in the scene.

"You're coming with us," the man in the white cap said, his tone leaving no room for argument.

"What is this about?" Richard demanded, his voice steady despite the fear that flickered in his eyes.

The man didn't answer. He grabbed Richard by the arm and yanked him forward. Richard struggled, but the other men closed in, their hands rough and unyielding.

"Leave him alone!" Dr. Saravanamuttu cried, her voice breaking. She reached out to grab her son, but one of the men shoved her back, sending her stumbling against the wall.

"Amma, it's okay," Richard said, his voice calm but strained. "I'll be fine."

The words were meant to reassure her, but they only made her heart ache more. She watched helplessly as they dragged him out of the house, his bare feet scraping against the floor.

The sound of the engine roared to life, drowning out her cries. She ran after the vehicle, her bare feet slapping against the cold pavement. "Bring him back!" she screamed, her voice hoarse with desperation.

The taillights disappeared into the darkness, leaving her standing in the doorway, her world shattered.

Dr. Saravanamuttu stood there for a long moment, the silence pressing down on her like a weight. Then, as if on autopilot, she turned and walked back into the house. Her hands trembled as she picked up the phone and dialed the first number that came to mind.

"Gamini," she said when the line connected. Her voice was barely above a whisper. "They've taken Richard."

Gamini Fonseka, the Deputy Speaker of Parliament, was a family friend and one of the few people she trusted. His voice was calm, almost too calm. "Don't worry, Manorani," he said. "Richard is in safe hands."

"What does that mean?" she demanded, her voice rising. "Where is he? Who took him?"

"I don't know," he admitted. "But I'll find out. Trust me."

She hung up the phone, her hands still trembling. The words "safe hands" echoed in her mind, but they brought no comfort. She sat by the phone, staring at it as if willing it to ring, as the hours stretched into an eternity.

The night passed in a haze of fear and helplessness. Dr. Saravanamuttu replayed the events over and over in her mind, searching for something she could have done differently. But the truth was as stark as it was cruel: there was nothing she could have done.

As the first light of dawn crept through the windows, she made a silent vow. She would find her son, no matter what it took. And if the men who had taken him thought they could silence her, they were gravely mistaken.

CHAPTER TWO

THE BODY

The sea was calm that morning, its surface shimmering under the pale light of dawn. Fishermen in Moratuwa, a coastal town south of Colombo, were preparing their boats for the day's work. The air smelled of salt and damp wood, and the rhythmic sound of waves lapping against the shore was a rare comfort in a country gripped by fear.

It was one of the fishermen, a wiry man named Sunil, who first saw it. At first, he thought it was driftwood, a dark shape bobbing in the water near the rocks. But as the tide carried it closer, he realized it was something else entirely.

"Over here!" he called out, his voice sharp with urgency.

The others gathered around, their faces grim as they pulled the body onto the sand. It was a young man, naked and lifeless, his skin pale and bruised. A gunshot wound marred his forehead, and his jaw was swollen and misshapen. There were bruises on his legs, and his private parts were swollen, a grotesque testament to the violence he had endured.

Sunil stepped back, his hands trembling. "We need to call the police," he said, though his voice lacked conviction. In these times, calling the authorities often brought more trouble than it solved.

One of the older fishermen shook his head. "They'll say we did it," he muttered. "Or worse, they'll make us disappear too."

But the body couldn't be ignored. It was too close to the village, too visible. Reluctantly, they sent a boy to fetch the police, and then they waited, their eyes fixed on the lifeless form before them.

The news spread quickly. By the time the police arrived, a small crowd had gathered on the beach, their whispers carrying a mix of fear and curiosity.

"Who is he?" someone asked.

"Looks like a journalist," another replied. "I've seen his face before."

The police officers, dressed in khaki uniforms and armed with rifles, pushed the crowd back. They worked with a detached efficiency, photographing the body and taking notes. But there was no urgency in their movements, no sign that they intended to treat this as anything more than another routine case.

One of the officers, a sergeant with a thick mustache, turned to his superior. "Should we take him to the morgue?" he asked.

The superior, a tall man with a stern face, nodded. "But don't make a fuss about it," he said. "We don't want this getting out of hand."

By midday, the body had been identified. It was Richard de Zoysa.

The news reached Dr. Saravanamuttu in the early afternoon. She had spent the morning making frantic phone calls, trying to find out where her son had been taken. Each call had ended in frustration, with vague reassurances or outright denials.

When the phone finally rang, she snatched it up, her heart pounding.

"Dr. Saravanamuttu?" a voice asked.

"Yes," she said, her voice trembling.

"This is Inspector Perera. I'm afraid we have some bad news."

The words hit her like a blow. She sank into a chair, her hand clutching the receiver as if it were the only thing keeping her upright.

"Your son's body was found this morning in Moratuwa," the inspector continued. "We're very sorry for your loss."

For a moment, she couldn't speak. The world seemed to tilt around her, the walls closing in. When she finally found her voice, it was barely a whisper. "Are you sure it's him?"

"Yes, ma'am," the inspector said. "We've confirmed his identity."

She hung up the phone without another word. The silence that followed was deafening, a void that seemed to swallow her whole.

The drive to the morgue was a blur. She sat in the back seat of a friend's car, her hands clenched in her lap, her mind racing. She had prepared herself for the worst, but nothing could have prepared her for this.

When she arrived, the coroner met her with a solemn expression. "I'm very sorry, Dr. Saravanamuttu," he said. "This way, please."

She followed him down a cold, sterile hallway, her footsteps echoing in the silence. When they reached the viewing room, he hesitated. "Are you sure you want to see him?" he asked gently.

"Yes," she said, her voice steady despite the storm raging inside her.

The sheet was pulled back, and there he was. Her son. Her beautiful, brilliant boy, reduced to this. His face was bruised and swollen, his body marked by the violence he had endured. She reached out to touch his face, but her hand stopped short.

This was not her son. This was a message, written in blood and pain.

The autopsy report confirmed what she already knew. Richard had been tortured before he was killed. The gunshot wound to his head was the final act, but the bruises and fractures told the story of what had come before.

The police, however, seemed uninterested in pursuing the case. They floated rumors that Richard had been involved with the JVP, a baseless claim meant to justify his death. They failed to follow leads, failed to take her testimony seriously, failed to act.

But Dr. Saravanamuttu refused to let her son's death be another statistic. She began to speak out, demanding justice, even as the threats against her began.

The public reaction was swift and furious. Richard de Zoysa was no ordinary victim. He was a journalist, a poet, a voice for the voiceless. His death was not just a tragedy; it was a symbol of everything that was wrong with the country.

Protests erupted in Colombo and beyond, with people demanding answers. International media picked up the story, shining a spotlight on the human rights abuses in Sri Lanka.

But for Dr. Saravanamuttu, the fight was personal. She had lost her son, but she would not lose her resolve. She would find the men who had done this, no matter the cost.

As she stood in the morgue, looking down at her son's lifeless body, she made a silent vow.

"This is not the end," she whispered. "I will not let them silence you."

CHAPTER THREE

THE MOTHER'S FIGHT

The house was quiet, but the silence was no longer comforting. It was oppressive, a constant reminder of the absence that now defined her life. Dr. Manorani Saravanamuttu sat at the dining table, a cup of tea untouched in front of her. The morning sunlight streamed through the windows, but it did nothing to warm her.

It had been three days since Richard's body was found. Three days of grief so profound it felt like a physical weight pressing down on her chest. But grief alone would not bring her son back, nor would it bring justice.

She had spent the last forty-eight hours making phone calls, meeting with lawyers, and speaking to anyone who would listen. The police had been dismissive, their investigation half-hearted at best. They had suggested, without evidence, that Richard had been involved with the Janatha Vimukthi Peramuna (JVP), the Marxist insurgent group that the government had been fighting for years. It was a convenient excuse, one that absolved them of responsibility.

But she knew the truth. Richard had been targeted because he had dared to speak out. His journalism, his poetry, his very existence had been a threat to those in power. And now, they wanted to bury the truth along with him.

Dr. Saravanamuttu knew she couldn't fight this battle alone. She began reaching out to Richard's friends, colleagues, and anyone who had been close to him.

One of the first people she called was Batty Weerakoon, a prominent lawyer and a family friend. Batty had known Richard for years and had always admired his courage. When she told him what had happened, his voice was filled with quiet anger.

"I'll take the case," he said without hesitation. "We'll make sure they don't get away with this."

His confidence gave her a glimmer of hope, but she knew the road ahead would be long and treacherous.

She also reached out to human rights organizations, both local and international. The International Commission of Jurists (ICJ) had already expressed interest in the case, and their observer, Anthony Heaton-Armstrong, was due to arrive in Colombo soon. His presence would bring international attention to the case, something the government would not be able to ignore.

The threats began almost immediately.

It started with anonymous phone calls. The first one came late at night, just as she was about to go to bed.

"Stop what you're doing," a voice said, low and menacing. "Or you'll end up like your son."

She hung up the phone, her hands trembling. But she refused to let fear control her.

The next day, a letter arrived in the mail. It was unsigned, the handwriting jagged and hurried.

"You're making a mistake. Drop the case, or you'll regret it."

She showed the letter to Batty, who frowned as he read it. "This is just the beginning," he said. "They're trying to scare you into silence."

"They don't know me very well, then," she replied, her voice steady.

But the threats didn't stop. She began noticing strange cars parked near her house, their occupants watching her with cold, unblinking eyes. Once, as she was walking to her car, she felt someone watching her. When she turned around, she saw a man in a dark suit standing across the street, his gaze fixed on her.

She refused to let them intimidate her. If anything, the threats only strengthened her resolve.

The first major step in the fight for justice was the inquest into Richard's death. It was supposed to be a straightforward process, a chance to establish the facts and hold those responsible accountable. But from the beginning, it was clear that the system was working against her.

The courtroom was small and crowded, filled with journalists, activists, and government officials. Dr. Saravanamuttu sat in the front row, her back straight and her hands folded in her lap. She wore a simple white sari, a symbol of mourning, but her expression was one of quiet determination.

The police presented their version of events, a story riddled with inconsistencies and outright lies. They claimed that Richard had been abducted by "unknown assailants" and that his death was likely the result of a dispute with the JVP.

When it was her turn to testify, she stood up and walked to the witness stand. The room fell silent as she began to speak.

"My son was not a member of the JVP," she said, her voice clear and unwavering. "He was a journalist, a poet, and an activist. He was taken from our home in the middle of the night by men who claimed to be police officers. I saw their faces. I heard their voices. And I will not rest until they are brought to justice."

Her testimony was met with murmurs of approval from the crowd, but the judge remained impassive. The inquest ended without any significant progress, but it was only the beginning.

A week after the inquest, Dr. Saravanamuttu was watching the evening news when she saw him. The man in the white cap.

He was standing in the background of a news report about a police operation, his face unmistakable. She froze, her heart pounding as the memories of that night came flooding back.

She called Batty immediately. "I've found him," she said, her voice shaking. "The man who took Richard. He's a police officer."

Batty came over that evening, and they watched the news report together. He agreed that the man in the white cap needed to be identified and questioned.

But when they brought the information to the police, they were met with indifference. "We'll look into it," the officer in charge said, his tone dismissive.

Dr. Saravanamuttu knew they wouldn't. If anything, they were likely protecting him.

The days turned into weeks, and the fight for justice became her sole focus. She spent her days meeting with lawyers, activists, and journalists, and her nights poring over documents and writing letters to anyone who might be able to help.

The threats continued, but she refused to back down. She had already lost her son. She would not lose her voice.

One evening, as she sat at her desk, she found herself looking at a photograph of Richard. It was one of her favorites, taken during a family trip to the beach. He was smiling, his eyes bright with life and laughter.

"I won't let them silence you," she whispered, her voice thick with emotion. "I promise."

CHAPTER FOUR

THE WHITE CAP

The days after Richard's death had blurred into one long, unending nightmare for Dr. Manorani Saravanamuttu. The grief was constant, a dull ache that never left her, but it was the anger that kept her moving. Anger at the men who had taken her son, at the system that allowed it to happen, and at the indifference of those who were supposed to protect him.

She had spent weeks trying to piece together what had happened that night. The police had been no help, their investigation sluggish and half-hearted. But she had her memories, and she clung to them like a lifeline. She remembered the man in the white cap, his pockmarked face, and the coldness in his eyes. She had told herself, over and over, that she would recognize him if she ever saw him again.

And then, one evening in May, she did.

It was a quiet evening, and the house felt emptier than ever. Dr. Saravanamuttu sat in the living room, the television on in the background. She wasn't paying much attention to the news broadcast until a familiar face appeared on the screen.

Her breath caught in her throat. It was him—the man in the white cap.

She leaned forward, her heart pounding, as the news anchor introduced him: Senior Superintendent of Police Ronnie Gunasinghe. The camera lingered on his face for a moment, and there was no doubt in her mind. It was the same man who had stood in her home that night, the man who had taken her son.

For a moment, she couldn't move. The room seemed to spin around her as the memories of that night came flooding back. She could hear the sound of heavy boots on the floor, the harsh voices of the men, and Richard's calm but defiant tone as they dragged him away.

She grabbed the phone and dialed Batty Weerakoon's number.

"I've found him," she said, her voice trembling. "The man who took Richard. He's a police officer. I just saw him on the news."

Batty listened carefully as she described what she had seen. "Are you certain?" he asked.

"I'm certain," she replied. "I'll never forget his face."

The next day, Batty filed an affidavit on her behalf, formally identifying SSP Ronnie Gunasinghe as one of the abductors. The affidavit was submitted to the magistrate overseeing the case, along with a request for an identification parade.

But the response from the authorities was far from encouraging. The police claimed that an identification parade was unnecessary, arguing that her identification was unreliable because it had occurred months after the abduction. They also pointed out that she had seen his name announced on television before she saw his face, suggesting that her identification was influenced by the broadcast.

Dr. Saravanamuttu was furious. "They're trying to discredit me," she told Batty. "But I know what I saw. I know it was him."

Batty nodded. "We'll keep pushing," he said. "They can't ignore this forever."

As the legal battle over the identification began, Dr. Saravanamuttu found herself haunted by questions about the man in the white cap. Who was he? Why had he been there that night? And what role had he played in her son's death?

Through her conversations with Batty and other allies, she began to piece together a picture of SSP Ronnie Gunasinghe. He was a senior police officer, known for his hardline tactics and his loyalty to the government. He had been closely involved in the operations to suppress the JVP insurgency, and his name was often mentioned in connection with human rights abuses.

"He's a dangerous man," Batty told her. "And he's well-connected. If he was involved in Richard's abduction, it's going to be very difficult to prove."

But Dr. Saravanamuttu refused to be deterred. "I don't care how difficult it is," she said. "I'm not going to let him get away with this."

The police's reaction to her identification was predictable but no less infuriating. They dismissed her claims, arguing that there was no concrete evidence linking Gunasinghe to the abduction. Instead of investigating him, they seemed more interested in protecting him.

When Batty requested an identification parade, the police delayed, claiming that it was unnecessary. When the magistrate ordered them to arrest Gunasinghe, they refused, arguing that there was insufficient evidence.

"It's like they're not even trying," Dr. Saravanamuttu said, her frustration boiling over. "They're treating me like I'm the criminal, not him."

Batty sighed. "This is how the system works," he said. "They're hoping you'll give up. But we're not going to let that happen."

As the case dragged on, it began to attract more attention, both locally and internationally. The media picked up on the story, and protests erupted in Colombo, with demonstrators demanding justice for Richard de Zoysa.

The International Commission of Jurists (ICJ) sent an observer, Anthony Heaton-Armstrong, to monitor the proceedings. His presence brought a sense of legitimacy to the case and put additional pressure on the authorities.

In his report, Heaton-Armstrong noted the systemic failures in the investigation. He criticized the police for their lack of urgency and pointed out the inconsistencies in their handling of the case. He also highlighted the broader context of disappearances and extrajudicial killings in Sri Lanka, describing Richard's death as part of a larger pattern of state-sponsored violence.

"The fact that Richard's body was recovered and identified is unusual," he wrote. "Most victims of abductions are never found. This case has exposed the cracks in the system, and it is imperative that those responsible are held accountable."

Despite the mounting pressure, the authorities continued to resist. The police argued that there was no concrete evidence linking Gunasinghe to the abduction, and the Attorney-General's office seemed reluctant to take any decisive action.

But Dr. Saravanamuttu refused to back down. She continued to speak out, giving interviews to the press and meeting with human rights organizations. She knew the risks—she had already received death threats—but she refused to be silenced.

One evening, as she sat at her desk, she found herself looking at a photograph of Richard. It was one of her favorites, taken during a family trip to the beach. He was smiling, his eyes bright with life and laughter.

"I won't let them silence you," she whispered, her voice thick with emotion. "I promise."

CHAPTER FIVE

THE INVESTIGATION

The investigation into Richard de Zoysa's abduction and murder was, from the very beginning, a labyrinth of delays, denials, and deliberate obfuscation. For Dr. Manorani Saravanamuttu, it was a battle not just against the men who had taken her son, but against an entire system that seemed determined to bury the truth.

The morning after the court hearing on June 1, 1990, where the magistrate ordered the arrest of SSP Ronnie Gunasinghe, Dr. Saravanamuttu sat in her living room, surrounded by stacks of legal documents. The order had been a small victory, but she knew better than to celebrate. The police had already made it clear that they had no intention of arresting one of their own.

Her lawyer, Batty Weerakoon, arrived shortly after breakfast, his face lined with exhaustion. He carried a folder of letters and affidavits, each one a testament to the uphill battle they were fighting.

"They're stalling," he said, dropping the folder onto the table. "The police are claiming there's not enough evidence to arrest Gunasinghe, even after your affidavit."

Dr. Saravanamuttu shook her head, her frustration mounting. "What more do they need? I saw him with my own eyes. I identified him."

Batty sighed. "It's not about evidence. It's about power. Gunasinghe is too well-connected. The Attorney-General's office is dragging its feet, and the police are doing everything they can to protect him."

In the midst of this stalemate, the arrival of Anthony Heaton-Armstrong, the observer appointed by the International Commission of Jurists (ICJ), brought a glimmer of hope. He was a tall, soft-spoken man with a sharp intellect and a deep commitment to human rights.

He met with Dr. Saravanamuttu and Batty in early July, just days before the next court hearing. Sitting in the small, cluttered office of the Bar Association of Sri Lanka, he listened intently as they recounted the events of the past few months.

"The delays, the lack of action, the threats—it's all part of a pattern," Batty said. "They want to wear us down, make us give up."

Heaton-Armstrong nodded. "It's a familiar tactic," he said. "But the fact that Richard's body was recovered and identified is unusual. Most victims of abductions like this are never found. That gives us an opportunity to push for accountability."

He promised to attend the upcoming court hearings and to document everything he observed. His presence, he said, would send a message to the authorities that the world was watching.

The courtroom was packed on July 5, 1990. Diplomats from several countries, including the United States, Germany, and Sweden, sat in the audience, their presence a silent rebuke to the Sri Lankan government. Journalists jostled for space, their cameras clicking as Dr. Saravanamuttu entered the room, flanked by Batty and Heaton-Armstrong.

The hearing began with the magistrate questioning the police about their failure to arrest SSP Gunasinghe. The lead investigator, a middle-aged officer with a perpetually nervous expression, stammered as he tried to explain.

"We... we believe there is insufficient evidence to proceed with an arrest at this time," he said.

The magistrate frowned. "Dr. Saravanamuttu has provided a sworn affidavit identifying SSP Gunasinghe as one of the abductors. What more evidence do you require?"

The officer shifted uncomfortably. "We... we are still investigating, Your Honor."

Batty stood up, his voice cutting through the tension in the room. "Your Honor, this is not an investigation. It is a cover-up. The police have had months to act, and they have done nothing. My client has received death threats, and yet she continues to fight for justice. The least the police can do is fulfill their duty."

The magistrate turned back to the officer. "I am ordering you to consult the Attorney-General and report back to this court within two weeks. If no action is taken, I will consider allowing the complainant's counsel to lead evidence in open court."

It was a small victory, but it felt like progress.

As the legal battle continued, the political climate in Sri Lanka grew increasingly volatile. The JVP insurgency had been crushed, but the scars of the conflict remained. Thousands of people had disappeared, their families left to wonder whether they were dead or alive.

Richard's case was unusual in that his body had been found and identified. Most victims of abductions were never seen again, their bodies burned or dumped in remote locations. The government's human rights record was under scrutiny, both domestically and internationally, and the case of Richard de Zoysa had become a symbol of the state's brutality.

Heaton-Armstrong documented these broader issues in his report, noting the parallels between Richard's death and the thousands of other disappearances. "The abduction and killing of Richard de Zoysa is hardly an unusual event in itself," he wrote. "What makes this case significant is the recovery of his body and the identification of those responsible. It has exposed the cracks in the system and the lengths to which the authorities will go to protect their own."

The closer they got to the truth, the more dangerous the situation became. Both Dr. Saravanamuttu and Batty received death threats on an almost daily basis. Letters arrived in the mail, their messages crude and chilling: "Stop now, or you'll be next."

One evening, as Batty was leaving his office, a man on a motorcycle sped past him, throwing a Molotov cocktail through the window. The fire was quickly extinguished, but the message was clear.

"They're trying to scare us," Batty said later that night, as he and Dr. Saravanamuttu sat in her living room, surrounded by the charred remains of the documents he had managed to save. "But we can't let them win."

Dr. Saravanamuttu nodded, her resolve unshaken. "They've already taken my son," she said. "They can't take my voice."

Despite the threats and the delays, there were moments of hope. Priya, a young journalist who had worked with Richard, began her own investigation into his death. She uncovered evidence linking SSP Gunasinghe to other disappearances, building a case that was impossible to ignore.

At the same time, international pressure on the Sri Lankan government continued to mount. Human rights organizations, diplomats, and journalists kept the spotlight on Richard's case, making it clear that the world was watching.

In late July, the magistrate announced that she would allow Batty to lead evidence in open court. It was a significant step forward, one that gave them a chance to present their case without interference from the police or the Attorney-General's office.

As they left the courtroom that day, Dr. Saravanamuttu felt a flicker of hope. The road ahead was still long and uncertain, but for the first time, it felt like justice might be within reach.

CHAPTER SIX

THE COURTROOM

The courtroom was packed. The air was heavy with tension, the kind that made every whisper seem louder than it was. Diplomats, journalists, and activists filled the benches, their presence a silent reminder that the world was watching. For Dr. Manorani Saravanamuttu, this was not just a legal battle—it was a fight for her son's memory, for justice, and for the truth to be heard.

The hearing on July 5, 1990, was a pivotal moment in the case. The magistrate had ordered the police to consult the Attorney-General about the arrest of SSP Ronnie Gunasinghe, but the police had done little to comply. Instead, they had doubled down on their claims that there was insufficient evidence to proceed.

As Dr. Saravanamuttu entered the courtroom, flanked by her lawyer, Batty Weerakoon, and the ICJ observer, Anthony Heaton-Armstrong, she felt the weight of the moment. This was her chance to present her case, to tell the court what she had seen that night. But she also knew that the forces arrayed against her were powerful and determined to discredit her.

The defense team, representing SSP Gunasinghe, was already seated. They were a formidable group, led by a senior lawyer with a reputation for ruthlessness. Their strategy was clear: to cast doubt on her identification of Gunasinghe and to argue that the case was politically motivated.

When the magistrate called her to the stand, Dr. Saravanamuttu took a deep breath and walked to the front of the courtroom. She had rehearsed this moment in her mind countless times, but now that it was here, the reality was overwhelming.

She began by recounting the events of February 18, 1990—the night her son was taken. Her voice was steady, but the pain in her words was unmistakable. She described the men who had entered her home, the man in the white cap who had led the group, and the moment Richard was dragged away.

"I will never forget his face," she said, her voice firm. "The man in the white cap. I saw him again on television in May. It was SSP Ronnie Gunasinghe."

The defense lawyer stood up, his expression calm but calculating. "Dr. Saravanamuttu," he said, "you claim to have identified my client on television. But isn't it true that his name was announced before his face appeared on the screen?"

She hesitated for a moment, then nodded. "Yes, that is true. But I recognized him immediately. His face, his pockmarked skin—it was him."

The lawyer pressed on. "Isn't it possible that your identification was influenced by the announcement of his name? That you were predisposed to believe it was him?"

"No," she said firmly. "I know what I saw. I would recognize him anywhere."

The defense team's strategy became clear as the hearing progressed. They sought to undermine her credibility, to paint her as a grieving mother desperate for someone to blame. They pointed out the delay in her identification, the lack of a pre-identification description, and the anonymous phone call she had received naming Gunasinghe as a suspect.

"Dr. Saravanamuttu," the defense lawyer said, "you have been under immense stress since your son's death. Isn't it possible that your memory of that night has been affected by your grief?"

She met his gaze, her voice unwavering. "My grief has not clouded my memory. It has sharpened it. I remember every detail of that night, and I will not be silenced."

Throughout the proceedings, Anthony Heaton-Armstrong sat quietly, taking notes. His presence was a reminder that this case was not just a domestic issue—it had drawn international attention.

During a break in the hearing, he spoke to Batty. "The defense is doing everything they can to discredit her," he said. "But her testimony is compelling. The challenge will be getting the court to act on it."

Batty nodded. "The magistrate seems sympathetic, but the system is stacked against us. The police and the Attorney-General's office are doing everything they can to protect Gunasinghe."

Heaton-Armstrong sighed. "It's a familiar story. But the fact that this case is being heard at all is significant. It's a chance to expose the truth, even if justice is slow to follow."

As the hearing continued, it became clear that the magistrate was in a difficult position. On one hand, the evidence presented by Dr. Saravanamuttu was compelling. On the other hand, the police and the Attorney-General's office were resistant to taking action against a senior officer like Gunasinghe.

When the defense argued that an identification parade was unnecessary, the magistrate pushed back. "If the identification is in question, then a parade should be conducted," she said. "It is the only way to resolve this matter."

The police, however, argued that a parade would be meaningless, given that Dr. Saravanamuttu had already identified Gunasinghe on television. The magistrate seemed unconvinced but stopped short of ordering the parade, instead instructing the police to consult the Attorney-General once again.

For Dr. Saravanamuttu, the hearing was both a victory and a setback. She had been able to tell her story, to name the man she believed was responsible for her son's abduction. But the lack of decisive action from the court was a bitter pill to swallow.

As she left the courtroom, she was surrounded by journalists. "Do you believe justice will be served?" one of them asked.

She paused, her expression resolute. "I believe in the truth," she said. "And I will keep fighting for it, no matter how long it takes."

Despite the challenges, there were moments of hope. The presence of diplomats and international observers sent a clear message to the Sri Lankan government: the world was watching. The media coverage of the hearing brought renewed attention to Richard's case, sparking protests and calls for accountability.

Priya, the young journalist who had been investigating Richard's death, approached Dr. Saravanamuttu outside the courtroom. "You were incredible in there," she said. "Your courage is inspiring."

Dr. Saravanamuttu smiled faintly. "It's not courage," she said. "It's love. Love for my son, and for the truth."

As the legal team regrouped that evening, Batty outlined their next steps. "We need to keep the pressure on," he said. "The magistrate is sympathetic, but she's limited by the system. We need to gather more evidence, find more witnesses, and keep the case in the public eye."

Heaton-Armstrong agreed. "The international attention is our greatest asset," he said. "We need to use it to push for action. This case has the potential to expose the broader issues of disappearances and state violence in Sri Lanka."

Dr. Saravanamuttu nodded. "They've tried to silence me," she said. "But I won't stop. Not until justice is done."

CHAPTER SEVEN

THE SHADOW OF JUSTICE

The courtroom battles had ended, but the fight for justice was far from over. For Dr. Manorani Saravanamuttu, the days following the hearings were filled with a heavy silence, broken only by the occasional phone call or the rustle of papers on her desk. The weight of the system's indifference pressed down on her, but she refused to let it crush her resolve.

The July hearings had been a turning point, but not in the way Dr. Saravanamuttu had hoped. The magistrate's reluctance to order the arrest of SSP Ronnie Gunasinghe, despite her compelling testimony, was a bitter reminder of the systemic resistance to accountability.

Batty Weerakoon, her lawyer, tried to reassure her. "The fact that the case is still being heard is a victory in itself," he said. "We've kept the spotlight on Richard's death, and that's more than most families in your position have been able to achieve."

But for Dr. Saravanamuttu, it wasn't enough. "They've turned my son's death into a political game," she said, her voice trembling with anger. "And they expect me to be grateful for scraps of attention."

The presence of international observers like Anthony Heaton-Armstrong had brought a measure of legitimacy to the proceedings, but it had also highlighted the limitations of external pressure. The ICJ report, released in August 1990, was scathing in its critique of the Sri Lankan authorities.

"The abduction and killing of Richard de Zoysa is hardly an unusual event in itself," Heaton-Armstrong wrote. "What makes this case significant is the recovery of his body and the identification of those responsible. It has exposed the cracks in the system and the lengths to which the authorities will go to protect their own."

The report called for an independent judicial inquiry into Richard's death, arguing that the existing legal framework was inadequate to address the systemic issues at play. But the Sri Lankan government, wary of international scrutiny, dismissed the recommendations as unnecessary interference.

For Dr. Saravanamuttu, the report was both a validation of her efforts and a stark reminder of the obstacles she faced. "They've acknowledged the truth," she said to Batty. "But what good is the truth if no one is willing to act on it?"

The months of fighting had taken a toll on Dr. Saravanamuttu's health. She had lost weight, her once-steady hands now trembling with exhaustion. Sleep came in fitful bursts, haunted by dreams of Richard and the men who had taken him.

One evening, as she sat alone in her living room, she found herself staring at a photograph of Richard. It was one of her favorites, taken during a family trip to the beach. He was smiling, his eyes bright with life and laughter.

"I'm sorry, my son," she whispered, tears streaming down her face. "I couldn't protect you. But I promise, I won't let them forget you."

Richard's case had become a symbol of the broader human rights crisis in Sri Lanka. The ICJ report noted that between 8,000 and 30,000 people had disappeared during the JVP insurgency, with the security forces often implicated in these abductions and killings.

"Almost invariably, the disappearances are absolute," the report stated. "Bodies are rarely identifiable as the killers take steps either to secrete them or to make identification impossible."

Richard's death was an exception, a "bungled job" that had inadvertently exposed the state's complicity in such crimes. But for every Richard de Zoysa, there were thousands of others whose families would never know what had happened to them.

Dr. Saravanamuttu began to see her fight as part of a larger struggle. She reached out to other families who had lost loved ones, offering them support and solidarity. Together, they formed a network of resilience, determined to keep the memory of their loved ones alive.

Despite the systemic failures, there were moments of hope. Priya, the young journalist who had worked with Richard, continued her investigation into his death. She uncovered evidence linking SSP Gunasinghe to other disappearances, building a case that was impossible to ignore.

At the same time, international pressure on the Sri Lankan government continued to mount. Human rights organizations, diplomats, and journalists kept the spotlight on Richard's case, making it clear that the world was watching.

One evening, Priya visited Dr. Saravanamuttu with a folder of documents. "I've found something," she said, her voice tinged with excitement. "It's not enough to convict him yet, but it's a start."

Dr. Saravanamuttu took the folder, her hands trembling. For the first time in months, she felt a flicker of hope.

The ICJ report concluded with a series of recommendations, including the establishment of an independent judicial inquiry into Richard's death and the creation of a special investigative team to handle cases involving allegations against the police.

"There appears to be a strong case for the setting up of an independent judicial inquiry," Heaton-Armstrong wrote. "Such an inquiry would at least establish some useful lessons for the avoidance of similar killings in the future and might point the way towards more effective police investigations."

But the Sri Lankan government showed little interest in implementing these recommendations. For them, Richard's case was an inconvenience, a reminder of the cracks in their carefully constructed facade of order and stability.

As the months turned into years, Dr. Saravanamuttu's fight for justice continued. She knew that the odds were stacked against her, that the system was designed to protect the powerful and silence the vulnerable. But she refused to give up.

"They've already taken my son," she said in an interview with an international journalist. "But they can't take my voice. As long as I'm alive, I will keep fighting for him."

Her words resonated far beyond Sri Lanka, inspiring others to speak out against injustice. Richard's death had become a rallying cry, a symbol of the resilience of those who refused to be silenced.

The chapter ends with a reflection on the nature of justice in a system as flawed as Sri Lanka's. For Dr. Saravanamuttu, justice was not just about holding her son's killers accountable—it was about exposing the truth, about ensuring that Richard's death was not in vain.

As she sat at her desk, writing yet another letter to a human rights organization, she thought of Richard's words: "The truth is worth fighting for, no matter the cost."

She smiled faintly, her resolve unbroken. The shadow of justice loomed large, but she would not stop until it was brought into the light.

www.ingramcontent.com/pod-product-compliance
Lightning Source LLC
Chambersburg PA
CBHW020517160726
47991CB00007B/3001